Pastoral

Other Books by Carl Phillips

From the Devotions
Cortège
In the Blood

Pastoral

Poems by
Carl Phillips

Graywolf Press
Saint Paul, Minnesota

Publication of this volume is made possible in part by a grant provided by the Minnesota State Arts Board through an appropriation by the Minnesota State Legislature, and by a grant from the National Endowment for the Arts. Significant support has also been provided by Dayton's, Mervyn's, and Target stores through the Dayton Hudson Foundation, the Bush Foundation, the McKnight Foundation, the General Mills Foundation, the St. Paul Companies, and other generous contributions from foundations, corporations, and individuals. To these organizations and individuals we offer our heartfelt thanks.

Published by Graywolf Press
2402 University Avenue, Suite 203
Saint Paul, Minnesota 55114
All rights reserved.

www.graywolfpress.org

Published in the United States of America

ISBN 1-55597-298-5

4 6 8 9 7 5 3

Library of Congress Catalog Card Number: 99-60738

Cover art: Reclining Pan, marble sculpture by Giovanni Angelo Montorsoli, The Saint Louis Art Museum

Cover design by Jeanne Lee

Acknowledgments

Some of the poems appeared in the following journals, for which all thanks to their editors:

Bostonia: "Animal"

Boulevard: "All art . . ."

Callaloo: "Clay," "Dearest Won," "Lay Me Down"

Chelsea: "Afterword," "A Fountain," "Hymn"

Excerpt: "Clap of Thunder"

Field: "Against His Quitting the Torn Field," "The Truth," "Unbeautiful"

Hayden's Ferry Review: "Black Box"

Indiana Review: "Billet-Doux"

The Journal: "Hour of Dusk"

New England Review: "Parable," "Wanted"

The New Republic: "The Gods Leaving"

The Paris Review: "Of That City, the Heart"

Parnassus: Poetry in Review: "Study, between Colors"

Pleiades: "Would-Be Everlasting"

Slate: "Gesture, Possibly Archaic"

TriQuarterly: "Abundance," "Autumn. A Mixed Music.," "The Kill,"
        "A Kind of Meadow," "Portage"

The Yale Review: "And Fitful Memories of Pan"

"Abundance" also appeared in *The Pushcart Prize XXIII: Best of the Small Presses,* edited by Bill Henderson, published by Pushcart Press, 1998.

"The Kill," "Retreat," and "The Truth" also appeared in *The New Bread Loaf Anthology of Contemporary American Poetry,* edited by Michael Collier and Stanley Plumly, published by University Press of New England, 1999.

I thank the John Simon Guggenheim Memorial Foundation for their invaluable encouragement, and for a fellowship which greatly assisted in the completion of this book. For the same reasons, all thanks as well to the Library of Congress for their award of a Witter Bynner Fellowship. Finally, my continued gratitude to Washington University for a summer travel grant and for the belief and support—at home and away—which helped these poems get written.

for Doug

—and to Robert

Contents

Not that they all are so; but that the most
Are gone to grass, and in the pasture lost.

George Herbert

———

         Come back. Come back.
Tell us of excess.
    What was the sign that limited?

Robert Duncan

I

A Kind of Meadow

— shored
by trees at its far ending,
as is the way in moral tales:

whether trees as trees actually,
for their shadow and what
inside of it

hides, threatens, calls to;
or as ever-wavering conscience,
cloaked now, and called Chorus;

or, between these, whatever
falls upon the rippling and measurable,
but none to measure it, thin

fabric of *this stands for.*
A kind of meadow, and then
trees — many, assembled, a wood

therefore. Through the wood
the worn
path, emblematic of Much

Trespass: *Halt. Who goes there?*
A kind of meadow, where it ends
begin trees, from whose twinning

of late light and the already underway
darkness you were expecting perhaps
the stag to step forward, to make

of its twelve-pointed antlers
the branching foreground to a backdrop
all branches;

or you wanted the usual
bird to break cover at that angle
at which wings catch entirely

what light's left,
so that for once the bird isn't miracle
at all, but the simplicity of patience

and a good hand assembling: first
the thin bones, now in careful
rows the feathers, like fretwork,

now the brush, for the laying-on
of sheen . . . . *As is always the way,*
you tell yourself, *in*

poems — Yes, always,
until you have gone there,
and gone there, "into the

field," vowing *Only until*
there's nothing more
I want — thinking it, wrongly,

a thing attainable, any real end
to wanting, and that it is close, and that
it is likely, how will you not

this time catch hold of it: flashing,
flesh at once

lit and lightless, a way
out, the one dappled way, back —

II

Clay

The shape of any thing
is the shape a line makes
around it.

So whatever my body can recall
of another's hands —
hard, spent upon it.

So whatever fossil
— a feather, a fern —
slate surrounds.

If there can be one, the shape
of any line
is its direction.

Shape, direction: the crosstrees.
That point where the two
cross has been narrative,

history — our story.
When did I choose
The Flesh, Wanting?

———

— *In Pompeii, it took ash to preserve the struggle against ash.*

Abundance

Not just the body — be it
as wild loam; as the loom with never a lack
of willing, schooled-enough

hands; or as steady
burning-glass beneath which, smoldering at
last, ah, give up.

But whatever bird, also,
bearing some equally whatever and now
irretrievable small life

where is home. The lip
too, that in its casual meeting with the glass
whose silvered rim

here is faded, here flakes, here
is gone,
meets all the other lips that once knew

and drank from the same glass —
an erotics
of cooled distance, all that history

has been, all that memory
is . . . .
Remember the buck, stepping free

of the dark wood,
of the wood's shadow, as if
just for you? And the antlers, you said simply,

branching like hands or
like trees.
I thought of the branching of mistake when,

presumed over,
forgotten,
on all sides at once it sports a fist

full of blooms.

What you must call the blooms,
call them. Prayers; these willed disclosures –

Clap of Thunder

Drove out to find one, found
instead a man single-fingering me
toward him.

> *Every stranger*
> *is an envoy of Fate's*
> *court* — not to receive whom . . . .

I followed. And — *There,*

'tis done with.

To return to the car,
to drive back to
home as I remembered it, what
else but these,

the unextraordinary motions
that define the life
we most live — we
are, most of us, mere context.

And then I stepped inside
of weeping.

And then my hands found,
classically,
my brow,
the usual pose adopted for

disbelief when one believes
that one has failed, has

failed one's art.

You will have seen how a sudden
wind shakes down
from the tree twice picked-over

still some last, lingering fruit, gone
ignored, or unsuspected.
Just so. — I began writing.

Dearest Won

Soon, I suspect, I shall be done with
the dove, and the steep rescue its wings
once, in storied flight unfolding, meant

promise of. Confess — if I grow used,
now, to a life all jazz-less blow and drag
of storm, it was not always so: before

I'd crossed a lover's trust, only to learn
I did not mind it; before I'd broken —
not a heart, but that as-yet deviceless,

still-apt-at-knee-to-buckle child that,
having looked every elsewhere, we turn
at last to the heart's winded field and

find, by a first snow amused, amazed,
finally — bewildered. In the scant,
hypnotic stagger to which here, in

the glowing walls of illumination, all
walking is shorn down, I need make
room for no one, with the exception of

my lately familiar but, for all that, no
less esteemed consort: praise. Though
restive as leaves, ever busy sustaining

then spilling the next brilliance, I shall
look to none to be lifted, evenings when
it is all I have wanted: to lie hollowed

out, crowned, gifted, and as pale . . . as
pale as — if damage could have flesh —
that flesh would be. In truth, regret, I

am like damage; be sure: I do not fail.

Study, between Colors

Now, everything comes
simple. Ladder, for
the reaching of what proves

hard to get to.
Dropcloth, guarantee
against – whatever falls.

You might have said.
The views, from this room,
are narrow, but go

far, I can see
not only the usual
lives careering towards end,

but some – haven't you
stood here? didn't you find
me among them? – some

more deliberately than others,
steeped in excess
of dull-headedness, or will,

or what for years I have
called hunger, as – as I
call it song,

what the doves in caves
lately grow fat on, swell,
the way waves do except

never breaking,
they fly like
waves never . . . .

I know –
You are blameless.
Earlier, how the sun through

no design of its own cast
seeming shrouds
on the floor's wood —

it passed, as the light
passes. The world is
sometimes that clean:

whom could I have
pointed to,
or what, and called thief?

Parable

There was a saint once,
he had but to ring across
water a small bell, all

manner of fish
rose, as answer, he was
that holy, persuasive,

both, or the fish
perhaps merely
hungry, their bodies

a-shimmer with
that hope especially that
hunger brings, whatever

the reason, the fish
coming unassigned, in
schools coming

into the saint's hand and,
instead of getting,
becoming food.

I have thought, since, of
your body — as I first came
to know it, how it still

can be, with mine,
sometimes. I think on
that immediate and last gesture

of the fish leaving water
for flesh, for guarantee
they will die, and I cannot

rest on what to call it.
Not generosity, or
a blindness, trust, brute

stupidity. Not the soul
distracted from its natural
prayer, which is attention,

for in the story they are
paying attention. They
lose themselves eyes open.

"All art . . ."

Routinely the sea,
unbuckling, out-
swells the frame it will

return to, be
held restively
by.

If there is a shadow
now, on the water, if
there are several,

somewhere are those that must
cast them, they will not
stay,

what does?
Our bodies, it turns out,
are not flutes, it

is unlikely that
God is a mouth with nothing
better to do than

push a wind
out, across us,
but we are human,

flawed therefore and,
therefore, shall suit ourselves:
Music

Hard Master
I called out,
Undo me, at last

understanding how
gift, any difficult
knot is — by

fingers, time, patience —
undone, knowing
too the blade by which

— if it means
the best, the most fruit — oh,
let the limbs be cut back.

Unbeautiful

Not blond not
well-fashioned not cut
from the enviably

blue silks, imagine, that
medieval fingers stitched into
streamers to be — by hands more fair, at

races — waved, to say *La, let
this horse win,*

let that one,

La,

———

as in Siena, where she
is treacherous — the course — a steep
bowl; the one thing sure: that

some of the horses will die,
or — broken now, and
wingless — be made to,

as the cobbled stones, bucketed,
hosed clean of blood, will
again shine.

Not any of these. More,

———

these flowers – their
stems. How,

by their own
burst crowns (flush-colored, color of

shame) conquered,

                      they bend just
shy of that angle things

find,

breaking.
        – Unbeautiful,

    —

and against
all wanting it, I do only what –
to whatever flourishes too well – ugly
has done

always. See here: these invisible

curves on the air, to mark
where a good was let go, a heart
jettisoned – that variously someone,
something else catches, does

not catch hold of: Wind   Hands   The water

    —

Don't cry.

> The artist is one who does not
> make mistakes.

Don't cry out.

> There was a silence, even, to
> the angels in their falling.

In trinities,

> In troops they fell.

Stars —

> Every one.

Hymn

Less the shadow
than you a stag, sudden, through it.
Less the stag breaking cover than

the antlers, with which
crowned.
Less the antlers as trees leafless,

to either side of the stag's head, than —
between them — the vision that must
mean, surely, rescue.

Less the rescue.
More, always, the ache
toward it.

When I think of death, the gleam of
the world darkening, dark, gathering me
now in, it is lately

as one more of many other nights
figured with the inevitably
black car, again the stranger's

strange room entered not for prayer
but for striking
prayer's attitude, the body

kneeling, bending, until it finds
the muscled patterns that
predictably, given strain and

release, flesh assumes.
When I think of desire,
it is in the same way that I do

God: as parable, any steep
and blue water, things that are always
there, they only wait

to be sounded.
And I a stone that, a little bit, perhaps
should ask pardon.

My fears — when I have fears —
are of how long I shall be, falling,
and in my at last resting how

indistinguishable, inasmuch as they
are countless, sire,
all the unglittering other dropped stones.

The Gods Leaving

That they carry away, with them,
vision — this isn't the worst of
the gods leaving: it's that they take

only half. There comes the hour
when — having lain long and favored
at the dark crossroads of Gift

and Desire; having as pliant
swans bested all arrows, no less
at ease with that wreckage than

with the glamour we have learned
to call pain given up to, until
wanted, a dream — we see it

was only, ever, our own bodies
by hands only our strong own
taken here, and here, down, ours

the mouths stalled at *Oh,* the eyes
clearing, enough to read or imagine
a reading for the shadows cast

to nobody's surprise by trees
theatrically there, shifting: *Don't
do this, don't do this* — always,

someone is too late . . . . At
that hour, because the gods aren't
indifferent, we rise into what,

already, is the new life — flat,
general, "never for such as
ourselves" — and it seems, at first,

just the old one: rain, the fact
of rain, so ordinary, stepping
into it, I did not think to cry out.

Black Box

The body, how
then it seemed the length of
beach into which the two
horses, beating
past us, struck their washaway
signs in that last light.

The soul, to be only
that to which so
little will, in
this world,
have been
granted, except waiting.

Ten pelicans,
exactly.

The grottoes, they
were of limestone.

The one who begged
Come,
I'm thirsty.

The one,
still whispering,
Come home.

Here,
where the skin has
reddened and —
somewhat — is swollen.

Here and,
where the cottonwood's
leavings cloud the water's
bank — there.

———

And if the fawn did not follow?

—

And if the doe,
missing nothing, climbing
the steep
slope like prairie,
disappears?

Lay Me Down

Lay me down.
     Let me.
Lay me down.
     Now.

As water upon
water, *think rain*
on particular waters:
Illyrian,

Potomac,
Mississippi —
My Barge?
My Skiff?

A paper boat across
the water of — *we have*
been places, times —
of one particular

and lost summer's
pool: dark,
and the only light
what the pool's lights

from below, *from*
beneath the water
cast through it and up to
each tree bent

toward it, and
the leaves accordingly
blue, lunar, a made
metal,

caustic, *as in*
or as if by flame
fired clean.
Now;

let me.
As snow upon,
into any vale,
that vale —

we have been
places, times —
where has always lain
historically

temptation,
we share that
history,
slim be it.

Sauvage,
Mon Sieur,
My Found and
Found Again

Star: for
as irradiant, though
I had otherwise —
I am swoon, so

am I blunder — yes,
predicted. You were:
Everything, they said.
I say it now.

Against His Quitting the Torn Field

Let him put his mouth in the dust — there may yet be hope.

Lamentations

"How, entering,
inside him, it became more
easy to believe I would not
breathe the same, it would not be
my life, breathing, breathed
— out, again, ever."

—

There was a bird, once,
like that. Or —

Or, shorn of bird — call only —
a calling-to that seemed
it would never end, be done
raveling.

It starts that way. Likely

—

it goes, somewhere else:

the mouth that says *You can do anything, here;*

the arm tattooed with —
as obviously as if this were
dream — the one word:
Paradise; all in a row, shut

against a frost that, even here, has
place, nine tulips —
seven; oh

and the peonies, or almost, each one
still a fist, which is to say, fat
with chance, or the hard
waking you will have forgotten bone also

———

can be. Somewhere else:

All house lights down.

Rustle of what no longer is required, being shed.

Sounds connoting struggle,
then —

silence? or
— like silence — resolve?

Lights up, on

the male lead, who has just found the body,
the body is someone's
he loved, he can see
it is dead; all the same
does he rock it, and rock it, poor

———

— bird?

There *was* one.
As there will be: yes, another.

Those birds fly well
which have little flesh,
and many feathers.

Though the flesh is
our enemy, we
are commanded to support it.

Of leaves, recall,
were the first garlands woven for
none other than, triumphant, the flesh.

——

      Thus, the shield.

          She set the clattering bronze down, before him.

III

And Fitful Memories of Pan

I. The Argument

The argument that rules out
excess must be
a slim one, for see

how easily, again, I have
ignored it. Or I
am willful or, worse, am

will crossed with damage,
a difficult truth I hold
long enough to know

generally its shape, then
let go. Am I not mostly
that thing the gods do

what they will with?
*A gift, something
for you*, they tell me, and

Go find it.
And always
I find something to take as

token, away, after,
this coin last time, its
face the blessing of sheer

wantlessness,
the curse of hunger its
obverse, rubbed naturally

past luster:
custom weighs
more than shine — as,

more than custom,
weighs loss, that field that,
if of late I step outside it,

I shall return to at that hour
when, if light could ache, most
achingly the light

tips across it.

II. Favor

Even from this distance, I can tell:
a man, clearly.
Gods cast no shadow.

Also, that he tires,
stops to rest, looks like

sleeping, or could use some.
How long he has been,
coming, how long it takes, just

to cross it, the lush
measure that — all summer — has

been these well-groomed,
well-fed grounds, the lake
unswum and gleaming, the light

catching, losing
the useless extravagance

that briefly the peacock
lifts, for tail, then drags, stiff
gown, behind, what it

means to thrive, in restraint.
All that way . . . that time . . . with

what message that all messages
aren't always?
Listen, I have a thing I must

tell you —
And expecting water. And

food, likely. Like
the others, of whom — if there is
some piece, still, of

remembering — let none call me
ungenerous. Always, the body

wagering —
up, through itself —
Give. What he wants, he shall have.

III. Nor Breath nor Heat

Nor stir.

> *As when — to those*
who with their bodies
too often

> *had been reckless, had*
as it were
made the lamp

> *on purpose*
fall, had made
a dark —

> *compassion*
came on wings that like
a reasonable question's

answer or a longish
story's plot took
their time

> *unfolding, but*
in time, with the steady
laboring by which

> *what does not*
know how close its own end is
beats toward it

> *he reached them,*
the heart's wrecked walls
from which, in color,

in profusion spill
those wrinkled (as if
waterlogged) thirsts,

the roses:
there, how still he lay,
— they

do, the lifeless.

IV. Dropped Flute

I do not say there weren't signs.

But when, deliberate
among the vines, his hands —
shaped by damage, fitted
for it — staked,
trellised the ones fallen,
brought to those not
past it some small, soft repair

— warming,
thickening, what did the air spell,
except salvage, thrive? If I forgot
harvest . . . .

          The gods are far,
we're told. Maybe. I do not
call the gods gone, nor
call it force, for — I swayed
easy, as

     will a field,
unto fire, from which
the shepherd, fast-
gathering, leading them,
saves the lambs, so they've
yet to reach it, their most
full, most slaughterable ripeness.

V. Dappled Shroud

Inside the man

stays — regardless, mere,
soft — a boy, the boy I
somewhere still
am, always,
the same, always: lying (for it is
easier, to say so) not

naked — dominoed,
in a light that comes
sifted, whatever
pattern that in the shaking
of leaves
wind, which too is

accident, does
not so much throw
down, it — lets fall . . . .
Not naked, no. Even
touching him, how wrong
is it to believe it is

not flesh I touch,
but something else,
thin, upon it that
shimmers,
and is flawed:
the ease with which, as

if willingly, the shroud
brooked intrusion,
was set to a trembling that
— like any song,
once mastered — how forget?
The notes:

The music:

IV

Afterword

In the long dreaming, the old gods are again
with us: some in the guise of ordinary
light through the green leaves they love

second best spilling, super-
intending; others as the small handfuls
of clothes that seemingly hold together

our bodies and then, as seemingly, do not –
as they fall away, like foes vanquished,
like the crumpled collapse

adoration assumes sometimes
in the wracked faces of believers put to
especially hard test. And

your body not your body any longer, nor mine
mine to give thought to, but the gods':
theirs, the hands that cast out; theirs,

the hands to fetch, surely, us back, so
a great ease
like death, poetry, both –

that place where the two make between them
a dove's tail, how each necessarily means
both the occasion for remembering and

the time finally for it, *I've lived that life,* each
singing. It's a dream, as I mentioned,
therefore from the dream – waking:

It's any morning. Coffee. The rinsed hours.
The holly tree, as if to shake itself from
its own dream,

rustling, bending, into the air its leaves
breaking against, snapping under the usual
scatter — birds, I mean,

and the squirrels lately.
Again, having waited for it, having been
afraid for it, that it wouldn't come,

I'm already writing the next poem; nothing's,
knock wood, the matter; somewhere you're still
with me, you're not with me —

Autumn. A Mixed Music.

Believe me, I would sooner
speak true —
And not of the leaves as the once-green

accomplices that, failing,
I shall most miss now,
October,

and how they sang to me
like water, singing
what was often enough

loss, eventually,
into choruses of *Something*
is lost, Something is still

gainable: You who call yourself
hunter, never lay
your bow down.

When was it all dreaming became
the one dream: myself
on the pier safe again, waving and

still waving, the body
at last separate — a vessel
steerable, but no longer

my hand steering —
and impossibly shackled
to it,

that god whose best trick
is to proffer madness as a balm
so sweet, who wouldn't

pick it up,
who wouldn't slather, in it,
his own body — hypnotic,

October . . . . And all the leaves
not failing — merely filling out entire
that space marked "Being Leaves."

And all the lives they covered, laid
bare now, finding elsewhere
to hide, to continue

variously toward an end that
comes always, however much a small
other thing beneath

> *Yes, inevitably, but*
> *not yet, there is still a distance*

continues . . . . Whatever edges, at

this lean hour, into view,
it is not the god;
is not, by other messenger, the desired

release granted; it isn't
the soul,
as too long imagined,

stepping into the visible world —

Listen: that doesn't happen in this world.

Of That City, the Heart

You lived here once. City — remember? —
of formerly your own, of the forever beloved,
of the dead,

       for some part of you, this part,
is dead, you have said so, and it is fitting:
a city of monuments, monuments to what is

gone, leaving us with our human need always
to impose on memory a body language, some
shape that holds.

       I can picture you walking
this canal, this park, this predictably steep
gorge through which predictably runs a river,

in which river, earlier today, I saw stranded
a bent hubcap, spent condoms, a cup by
someone crushed, said *enough* to, tossed . . . .

City in which — what happened? or did not
happen? what chance (of limbs, of spoils)
escaped you?

       And yet . . . . I have sometimes
imagined you nowhere happier than here, in
that time before me.

       I can even, from what
little you have told me, imagine your first
coming here, trouble ahead but still far,

you innocent   of disappointment, still
clean. In those historical years preceding
the sufferings

       of Christ, there were cities
whose precincts no one could enter unclean,
be their stains those of murder, defilement

of the wrong body, or at what was holy some
outrage. There were rituals for cleaning;
behind them, unshakable laws, or —

they seemed so . . . . But this city is not
ancient. And it is late inside a century
in which clean and unclean,

                        less and less,
figure. At this hour of sun, in clubs of
light, in broad beams failing, I do not

stop it: I love you. Let us finally, un-
daunted, slow, with the slowness that a
jaded ease engenders, together

                        step into
— this hour, this sun: city of trumpets,
noteless now; of tracks whose end is here.

Wanted

In dream, every one of the mind's lakes is
Lake Como, and him entering and entering
until, finally, inside it, he is the far — then

the more far — act of flesh performing one
languorous, sure stroke after another, which
is swimming, but is also a kind of signaling,

as across those blue and otherwise unyielding
waters returns only sign: *chance bird, I've
lost you.* And what's the difference, now

that you've found yourself once more inside
these waking hours whose silence, notice,
cups perfectly the sound of fruit by laws of

weight and time dropping into a green that
could mean: what, grass? Or only time,
grass-redundant? You walk as usual, down

streets with landed names like Winchester,
Corey, Gray, finally Marlborough, once his
favorite, you remember, for its magnolia-ed

giving up of itself into the Public Gardens
where the swans are: they veil the water in
wakes that idly recall the less visible wake of

him turning toward sleep and away, done
with the motions of love, of come . . . . It's
only later, in the sudden, long-necked grace

of them ascending, disappearing, that you
can understand the swans for what they are
— the necessary clues to lead you nowhere,

they refuse you all assistance, save that
oldest trick you know already, have always
used, elimination: *not him, not him, not him . . . .*

Would-Be Everlasting

There is a sea there. Nobody looks at it, or rarely, and even then only as, in
    bed, one turns
occasionally from reading to see the beloved of course there, and of course
    breathing, his
body asleep rises, falls — what different thing is expected?

There, when a body dies, the bereaved assemble and, filling glasses with the
    local drink —
a syrup whose taste, if desire could be made into liqueur, would be desire, as
    bracing as it,
as undiluted with guarantee — they toast over and across the dead. Then
    they leave:

there are other bodies. Prone on the sand, and except for oil naked, each
    making of brow
and muscle a half-nacreous, half-striated dark vow or request, they show
    what it means,
there, to worship — their glossed mouths too, kept open so as to let whatever
    comes to fill

fill them. For everything there, empty, must be filled, or let go. Even the
    birds understand
this, by whose filling of all the spaces where leaves are no longer, the failing
    tree remains
useful; the ax, for now, passing —

They've a saying there for the heartsick. They say: *However fair still to look
    at, he bears a*
thorn in his throat. They believe the throat is a sieve woven of wounds both
    incurred and
escaped from. By this logic all speech becomes, unsparingly, remembrance:
    we sing, and

we are betrayed . . . . How much
was true? Not native to it, how much has from that country been my own
rough translation?

Billet-Doux

Nobody lied; left to themselves, the waves
do find a pattern, and it is an old one,
yes: one roar,

         another. And, in between,
a silence only relative — narrow, but
not so narrow that it can't hold, too,

at the window, the sound of bees making
of an act like thumping against glass or
a screen   any same thing,

            and always —
the one habit that it is. How many times
have I taken you into

          my body? is neither
a steep bill nor the money, out of nowhere
rising, with which to pay it,

          but — as
if as tangible — is a question, that comes
toward and then

        leaves me. From mountains
only a couple of hours, not worlds away,
you write of the trees, "each is a lesson

in how to live half-broken," how to draw
a life from what at first — rock, and
the soil just as hard — seems unable to

give any. You have given the flowers new,
simpler names: Little Purple, Little Yellow,
Little Green . . . .

       Eventually, any bruise —
however bad — lifts, disperses. I have
always admired that about the flesh. I

admire you. If I always want to remember
to say so more — then forget — I still want
to remember.

        I'm not so sure I want as
much, anymore, to understand where we are
different . . . .

        Just yesterday, in the wake
of a day's rain, I looked out and saw what
I'd never seen,

          a double rainbow. Had you
been here, you would have taken a picture,
being a man who takes

              pictures. I thought
Only if I tell him will he say he missed
something; and I was sorry: aren't phenomena,

if that's what you want to call them,
brief, in general — slight, compared to
the ordinary life

          that meanwhile manages,
beneath, to go on? You would say it
depends, I suppose — who is asking,

who is asked. You'd probably remind me
there are other things besides rainbows,
ask what about earthquakes,

             or those
moments — *like* earthquakes — when what
matters most is, suddenly, location;

when the words of least value, because
also the most used, come down to *help* and
where are you —

          The sea is everything,
this morning: blue luck, a stone hand;
coins, that all but give themselves up.

A Fountain

Therefore, not this ocean's
ordinary enough wave and
wave,
     but like it,
               but more vertically

a fountain

crests,
then
    falling upon,
               feeds
itself,
    to be a fountain is to flourish,
but in stasis, to be
              a fountain is to
maybe not know what it means
to live —
      to flash, even — by self-
crippling, but it
is to mean that.

        I say so,
because I can.
        I can, because
I know now, because

it is the rare lesson that escapes me,
the same for memory:

           when I fell
into the beautiful (word,
for once, not overused, as he
was not)
      into the beautiful stranger's
wanting, when I fell not for the
first time, it
      was for the first time
haltingly and more than half

(promise)

uncertainly
I did so —

      Crests.

And falls.

      We're here, again.
                We're
at the beach.
      You're where you've
been, the water.

You leave the water.

The water leaves your body like what knows
it can afford to, at last.

For aren't there others.

You're coming
      closer. The body — *gleams.*

Animal

The shadow, leaving

the tree's shadow is —
with a single wing surrendered
at its mouth — the cat: don't

turn it off. To be animal
is to make constantly
room for what opposes, to

accommodate, or
fail fully. Thus the bird,
its folded story.

Though it is human,
less to give to the doomed
rescue, than to want to —

less to want to than to
regret the helplessness that
true regret stands for —

stop. To be animal means
never to court, once
recognized, what's dangerous.

To be human: the recognition,
the coming closer, to think
surely a way will

open up, by which we
shall outswerve what could
undo us. Wittingly, every moment,

somebody somewhere who
isn't a child is, like one,
offering trust and flesh,

as if together the two might
shield against the hunger
given into, should something —

nerve, hunger itself, the trusted
stranger gone from human to pure
animal, flesh — turn.

Thus, occasionally, disaster.
More ordinarily, thus
avoidable mistake avoided

badly. Though to be human
involves promise, I
won't promise — and don't

you, at this hour. The light
leaving. The cat rapidly
less visible. Anything

likely, given distance:
what was always the case.
From the cat's mouth,

equally a wing
single and hanging; a shadow
trapped there. Beating

there.

Portage

No longer that country
the vision came from,
his body was

his body, already bringing me
gifts from a dead world:
that last morning,

husk of a horseshoe
crab, for remembering
there was once

a prehistory, yes; the blue
half-shells of mussels
for beauty when it comes

small, pearled, and minus
instruction. So many relics,
without the power of

so many relics . . . . Let him
carry out of this life what
he can. Myself,

I am taking this over
and over retrieved and dropped
chain that, across waters

uncertain, one beacon's light
made with another's: *Where
are you   Here*   Again,

Where   I take also – have
kept room for – the doves
once, twice: the initial

wind-snapped wash of
their wings toward ascent;
then the doves visibly

themselves, with — because of
a name they don't ask for —
the unswallowable mourning

for a loss that never shows,
forever stuck inside
their excellent, downed throats.

Hour of Dusk

Finally, hero means only having
with more distinction, nerve, or
notoriety than the rest of them

passed through. We say of one
that around his robe he placed
dried pomegranates, bells, so that

where he walked was a music;
another, story has it, seemed little
different from a young Lebanon

cedar in the midst of, everywhere,
palms; to remember a third, we
have only to think scent, distilled

fresh by the perfumer's petal-stained
hands – he becomes ours . . . . It's
over, again: the dropped stole of

my body, the blade falling of his,
on it, the ritual tearing of (O, I shall
miss it) the body's sheer, notional

fabric that, already, begins stitching
itself whole toward a next time it
can't know, but presumes. Hour

of dusk, come. Sky of songbirds,
come with it, mouths gaped not
in song but for those night-flying

insects that now, but too early, too
readily, ascend. Like everything
living, they are flawed, and they

must die. Hour when most palpable
– the always, unspooling . . . . It is
why I sing for them, I think. That

it must, all of it, go. Insect. Bird.
The event between them that – is
need until, unflinchingly, it isn't.

Gesture, Possibly Archaic

Careful   confident   both, and

prone, the two of them, to
laughing, they got
into the boat.

One put his hands to the oars
there, and the boat
left.

      The other, raising
against wind his collar,
freed unmeaningly a litter of thin

blossoms that *could be*
peach, or the little apple that — for
how slow it is, coming

sweet — is called
reluctance . . . .
                        The blossoms spilled

first onto wind, then
onto the water behind the boat, and
for a while

the water flared
outside of a stillness it
would return to:

A boat meant nothing in that country;
the men won't, either
one of them, be missed —

Retreat

The sea and then, before it, the salted
meadow of sea-hay, the meadow
graven by narrow channels, the more

easy, once, to gain entry, farmers
sailoring into — to cut again down —
the meadow, to harvest the blue, the

green hay which is blond now, which
will for months stand for *Sleeping, Let
be,* the kind of abandon that is endurable

because its ending, if not yet visible,
is nevertheless sure, as much anyway
as all promises: believe them, or

don't believe them, and — then what?
That's history, about the farmers.
Come spring, then summer, the boats

that come instead will be for finding
pleasure because, simply, it's findable
here, and still free, even if, just now,

who will say so? Nobody's here. In
the narrow channels, no pleasuring
boats, either. A single and wooden

dock, yes, but opening out into a space
in which nothing drifts tethered and
waiting, unless memory — what some

plash of want or of need, idling briefly,
makes appear there — counts, waiting.
From inside the meadow, the fidget of

darkness that was, all along, birds
lifts abruptly, assembles: first a shield
thrown, too soon, too recklessly aloft,

then any door by a storm opened, in a
wind swinging, that someone — whom
nobody sees, whom nobody thinks,

therefore, to thank — passes, and —
not tenderly, just — responsibly, pulls
shut. The body first. Then the soul.

for Mark and Randy

The Truth

And now,
the horse is entering
the sea, and the sea

        holds it.

Where are we?

Behind us,
the beach,
      yes, its

scrim,
    yes, of
          grass, dune, sky — Desire

goes by, and though
it's wind of course making
the grass bend,

       unbend, we say
it's desire again, passing
us by, souveniring us with
gospel the grass, turned
choir, leans into,

      Coming —
Lord, soon.

Because
it still matters, to say something. Like:
the heart isn't

     really breakable,
not in the way you mean, any more
than a life shatters,

— which is what
dropped shells can do, or a bond sworn to,
remember, once

couldn't, a wooden boat between
unmanageable wave and rock or,
as hard, the shore.

The wooden boat is
not the heart,
the wave the flesh,
the rock the soul —

and if we thought so, we have merely been
that long
mistaken.

Also,
about the shore: it doesn't
mean all trespass
is forgiven, if nightly
the sand is cleared of
any sign
we were here.

It doesn't equal that whether
we were here or not
matters,
doesn't —

Waves, because
so little of the world, even
when we say that it has
shifted, has:

same voices,
ghosts, same
hungers come,
stop coming —

Soon —

How far the land can be found to
be, and
of a sudden,
                sometimes. Now —
so far from rest,
should rest be needed —

Will it drown?

The horse, I mean.

And I — who do not ride, and
do not swim

And would that I had never climbed
its back

And love you too

V

The Kill

The last time I gave my body up,

to you, I was minded
briefly what it is made of,
what yours is, that

I'd forgotten, the flesh
which always
I hold in plenty no

little sorrow for because — oh, do
but think on its predicament,
and weep.

We cleave most entirely
to what most we fear
losing. We fear loss

because we understand
the fact of it, its largeness, its
utter indifference to whether

we do, or don't,
ignore it. By then, you
were upon me, and then

in me, soon the tokens
I almost never can let go of, I'd
again begin to, and would not

miss them: the swan
unfolding
upward less on trust than

because, simply, that's
what it does; and the leaves,
leaving; a single arrow held

back in the merciless
patience which, in taking
aim, is everything; and last,

as from a grove in
flame toward any air
more clear, the stag, but

this time its bent
head a chandelier, rushing
for me, like some

undisavowable
distraction. I looked back,
and instead of you, saw

the soul-at-labor-to-break-its-bonds
that you'd become. I tensed
my bow:

one animal at attack,
the other — the other one
suffering, and love would

out all suffering —

Notes

The epigraphs: Herbert's "The Church-Porch" and Duncan's "The Propositions."

> "The Propositions" by Robert Duncan, from *The Opening of the Field.*
> Copyright © 1960 by Robert Duncan. Reprinted by permission of New
> Directions Publishing Corp.

"All art . . ."

The title is from a line of Robert Hayden's "The Tattooed Man."

Against His Quitting the Torn Field

> "Those birds fly well which have little flesh" and "Though the flesh is
> our enemy, we are commanded to support it" originally appear in part
> three (pages 66 and 69, respectively) of the thirteenth-century work
> *Ancrene Wisse: Guide for Anchoresses* as translated by Hugh White,
> published by Penguin UK, 1993.

> The final line of the poem is Homer's: *Iliad* XIX, line 12 (translation
> mine).

Hour of Dusk

> The descriptions of heroes in stanzas 2-5 are after the descriptions –
> in *Ecclesiasticus* – of the heroes Aaron (45:9), Simon (50.12), and
> Josiah (49:1), respectively. See *The New English Bible with The Apoc-
> rypha: Oxford Study Edition,* published by Oxford University Press,
> 1976.

Parable

> The ability to attract fish by means of ringing a bell is attributed to
> the sixth-century French saint, Guignolé.

> It is the late sixteenth/early seventeenth-century philosopher
> Nicholas Malebranche who first posits the paying of attention as the
> natural prayer of the soul, and it is Walter Benjamin who phrases it so
> succinctly. I thank Geoffrey Hill for directing me to the work of both.

CARL PHILLIPS is the author of three previous books of poetry, *From the Devotions*, *Cortège*, and *In the Blood*. He has received prizes and fellowships from the Guggenheim Foundation and the Library of Congress, and has been a finalist for both the National Book Award and the National Book Critics Circle Award. He teaches at Washington University in Saint Louis.

This book was designed by Donna Burch. It is set in Rotis type by Stanton Publication Services, Inc., and manufactured by Bang Printing on acid-free paper.